DANCING THE TIGHTROPE

New Love Poems by Women

Barbara Burford: Blackwoman; forty-two; Zami. She has published a collection of short stories, *The Threshing Floor* (1986) and her poems have appeared in *A Dangerous Knowing: Four Black Women Poets* (1984).

Lindsay MacRae was born in 1961 and has studied drama, film and television. She has played the saxophone in several bands, worked for Vatican Radio as a newsreader and is a regular performer of her work on the cabaret circuit. Her poetry has been published in *No Holds Barred* (1985), *Angels of Fire Anthology of Radical Poetry in the Eighties* (1986) and *Purple and Green* (1985). She works as a journalist/ scriptwriter and lives with friends in London.

Sylvia Paskin is a writer/lecturer in film, literature and feminism, and co- edited the *Angels of Fire Anthology of Radical Poetry*.

DANCING THE TIGHTROPE

New Love Poems by Women

Edited by Barbara Burford,
Lindsay MacRae and Sylvia Paskin

PETER BEDRICK BOOKS

New York

First American edition published in 1988 by
Peter Bedrick Books, Inc., New York by
arrangement with The Women's Press, Ltd. , London

First published by The Women's Press, Ltd. 1987

The title of this book is inspired by a line from
"Kite-flying" by Kath McKay

Library of Congress Cataloging-in-Publication Data

Dancing the Tightrope.

   1. Love poetry, English—Women authors.
   2. English poetry—20th century. I. Burford,
   Barbara. II. Macrae, Lindsay. III. Paskin, Sylvia.
   PR1184.D36 1988 821'.914'080354 87-33352
   ISBN 0-87226-177-8
   ISBN 0-87226-201-4 (pbk.)

Manufactured in the United States of America

The paper used in this book complies with the Permanent
Paper Standard issued by the National Information Stan-
dards Organization (Z39.48-1984).

10 9 8 7 6 5 4 3 2 1

Contents

Preface

While women writing today no longer feel the need to learn their art from their male predecessors, certain conventions exist that have proved hard to overcome and nowhere else is this more evident than in love poetry.

The terrain of male poets down the ages is littered with references to women – as unattainable and therefore worshipped as 'goddesses', as virgin prey, as hapless victims and fatal tormentors. We certainly needed the 'new psychic geography' Adrienne Rich spoke of in *When We Dead Awaken!* It is the aim of this anthology to map out new territory. We have been listening and waiting and observing in silence and in shadow for a long time, and in the last ten years or so there has been a marvellous and brilliant flowering of women's writing. This anthology is not like others and it is also very much a beginning. We wanted to create a space for women writing poetry about sexual love – woman to woman and woman to man. We have made a selection of poems from women of a wide range of cultures and backgrounds.

Our selection can give only a glimpse of the richness, variety and strength which is women's writing today – particularly about this most simple, most intense, most complex and most delicate of human emotions. The poems are all very different – they reflect different moods, styles and attachments – and yet they all connect. They share a common sensibility, a sensibility which is complex, subversive and unorthodox. Every time we fall in love, we join the resistance movement. Let the struggle continue . . .

Barbara Burford, Lindsay MacRae, Sylvia Paskin

DANCING THE TIGHTROPE

New Love Poems by Women

Breaking days

Breaking days
are quiet. Rain
trickles to the swelling
of a huge ache of

a waiting muffled the
appearance of serenity
but stuck
in flight as sheep

scared up a hill
from oh oh oh
the glass moment hard
and bare a

decadence of coldness. And
now I make you
a vast house a
quiet darkness an

absence gone
and not cared for. What
momentous removal!
An emptiness

of walls they fall in and
castigate. Where
windows looked out
to grass, heard

rain softly falling this
leg thrusts
an accusing
after hurt. No

white sheet
can sweeten away no

rain
can ever falling day

after day wash out that
harsh cancer. It
bleeds out. And
now the rain is ceased

the soft insistent hushing has
gone away the clouds
have emptied themselves they have
shed their water. The day

has broken open and
particular sounds
take place. There is
a shout of light, it

lies upon the table barred
by the sash
of shadow, and the black thread
is electric across fields, they

are sombre sogged
by always rain and
this body soft
as a presence of flesh, white

and speckled
lays around and
a laziness of love dissolves
a bed rock of lies.

Sara Boyes

Stars

We stand facing each other, our
flesh flatters our mirrors. And the stars

shoot darting
all through our dark sky. Fold our dark sky

about us
now our quiet passion is pulsing.

Sara Boyes

Bathing

Water fills
to the brim. It has
a green essence an
emerald longing. Such

seaweed floats
here   softness is
a cushion under soap. This
is a close tub   holds.

A sucking
takes place, all the world
sucks and drinks
dancing drunk in a glory. There

is a wet skin it
can be pulled down, at
the bottom there only
the dregs or

can blunt up
secreting precious juices and
broad and broad
are these planes. Such

a straight nape
to be caressed such blunt
buts and cliffs jut
out such

bigness to be had be
in. I shall go
under   find
ways to breathe under there.

Sara Boyes

Manumission

There. I set you free.
For, I could no longer risk dying,
and you unborn.
Could not condemn you to the last
dim fizzling of my mind.
Not you. Alive from my earliest thoughts;
changing gender, shape, colour.
Not to my whim,
but your delicate sense of my need.
There I set you free.
But will you stay?
Just for a while.

There. I let you go.
Let you flow out from my fingertips;
in ink, in blood, in tears.
Such a birth –
no succour needed.
Take your substance as you will.
Wink at me from the postman.
Glare at me from the cat.
Sing descant to my shaky treble.
Push me back into the human race.
There. I let you go.
Go. Else you'll take me with you.

Barbara Burford

5

You

You move
like the sound of pipes
in a mountain starlit
night.
With a centred stillness
round which all is
magic, and lithe motion.

You taste
like midwinter's memory
of hot sun on bare
skin.
Secret amber honey under
my tongue. Like the jewelled
coolness of a handful of
pomegranate prisms.

You are
my beginning place,
the blood in my veins.
Intimate but with a
wild unknowing power
that shakes the soul.

Barbara Burford

September Blue

O blue is such a fatal colour,
September blue.
There was I
drowned deep in a life
like blackstrap molasses.
Only the occasional tiger flash
of an enraged golden eye
to show where I still lived.
Then deep, delayed,
September blue.

Feet first
I emerged, like a breech birth
or dripping canal drowning,
ropes burning my ankles.
Trying to breathe my strangling life.
Airless.
Curling, twisting,
I glimpse small square hands,
a downy cheek.

Now I'm Christmas drunk
on September blue
I dream a dream
too wide for my bed.
Clench my teeth on a song
too big for my mouth.

When I am gone.
When life has rendered me
down to my various elements:
Wife, mother, scientist.
And left my bones
beached on some Antarctic shore.
Look in the clutched bones
of my left hand.

You will find the silver tear
I cried for joy of loving you.

Barbara Burford

Scheherazade

I am Scheherazade,
am I not?
The weaver of words,
teller of tales.
Yet it is you that
stays my executing hand,
that speaks on the side
of myself.

I should enspell,
cast a glamour.
Yet you place your
body between me
and my destructive emotions.
Between me and the upright
sarcophagus that was
once my ivory tower.

Across a grey plain,
dirty with pain.
Along the sea bottom
silted with years of doubt.
I swim, walk, run
haltingly,
sometimes in circles,
but always towards you.

So, poor ragged
weaver of tales,
I stand exposed.
Where I sought to enchant,
I stand ensorcelled.

Barbara Burford

Reflections

Today the sky hangs just above my brows.
Packed heavy with the promise of snow.
Held back only by
the bare, black, many-fingered
branches of the cherry tree.

My reflection, no longer distorted
by your expectations,
watches me from the darkening window.
A woman reclaiming those spaces
that, foolish profligate,
she had given over to someone else.

Yes, the connections still remain,
thin threads of awareness.
No longer strangling, enmeshing.
While inside me, whole constellations
arch across the night-dark
promise of my future.

Yet, sometimes I hear your voice
silvering the night.
Though you are months gone;
your voice, your scent,
the very taste of you, remain.
And I.

Barbara Burford

Penelope

I see her on a beach
with whitened shells and bones
on honey coloured sand,

women with her. 'The sea
is yours my lord, but see
the beach is ours. We walk
here often in the evening
and gather shells and stones
and weeds and dreams to weave;

the beach is ours, and all
the time there is is ours.
We hear each others' dreams
and weave the colours
into cloth and daydreams.

When you will return
my lord, there will be
feasting, storytelling, love,
and much will be regained
that by your absence
we have lost;

but love, when you return
then something will be lost
that we have found.'

Janet Dubé

Happily ever after,
from the story of the same name

He raised his sword
and firmly struck
at the gnarled and ancient wood.
It was harder than he'd thought;
it took several days to clear
the vast entanglement;
but at last he'd made a path
and broken down the door
and she was lovely.
They made the palace
into a sort of museum,
and had the gardens properly landscaped.
He soon learnt to understand her
and to love her gentle dependency.
They went visiting relatives
who all spoke so differently anyway
that the language didn't seem to matter.

Later, affairs of state
took up much of his time.
Her attempts at sewing
were almost disastrous
and she couldn't learn the language.
One day, when he was away,
she went back to the old palace,
climbed up to the attic
and fell asleep again.

When they finally heard from him
he sent some money, and wrote
that he'd taken up with seven small miners
and would be gone some time.

The staff were so relieved
that they didn't even bother to answer the letter.

Janet Dubé

No one's land

Maybe this is the final battle
in the war between the man
and the woman, this great
and petty careful fight
between all the men and
all the women that we know:
someone, somewhere
is drawing up statements
for swearing and signing,
final surrender, honourable
peace. We have to go on
fighting, till the last break
or baby, fuck or hope, and after
that, in unarmed combat
of the oldest kind. I can
find no words or actions
that have not been used
before. I give myself up,
and only hesitate this side
of treachery, and only just.

Beyond this no one's land
I seek another, where
in being waywardly faithful
to just ourselves, we are
perfectly faithful
to each other. Till then
we mustn't promise anything.

Janet Dubé

Reflections

she saw the world from inside out, he saw it upside down:

she was a geophysicist,
he was a white-faced clown.

They had much in common;
for example, both enjoyed the moon,

she from an interest in its rocks,
craters, and other messages;

he from an interest in its tides,
and its reflection of his own white face.

Of their children, according
to the laws of heredity,

one played a clarinet, one danced a minuet
and two were fortune-tellers.

Other children came up in the garden,
dressed as lilac, broom, or apple trees.

All were unable to pass examinations,
but some wrote songs, some played,

and were able to amuse their parents,
as, aging, unable to speak to one another,

they watched the moon together,

he from an interest in its geophysics,
she for its reflection of her own white face.

Janet Dubé

Matauwhi Bay V

I lie on my side,
Knees drawn up
In the dull pain men never know.

My cat licks my fingers,
Then jumps down from the narrow bed
To sprawl on cool white linoleum.

When the tide is full,
I will take my kahawai skeleton
Down to the wharf for bait

And bring us back sprats.

Amanda Eason

Some Things

Some things
like patched sheets
I want back when you go

Others
like compliments
keep

their fragrance lingers.

Amanda Eason

I dreamt you went

I dreamt you went
To Ecquador
And didn't stop to tell me.
You left on golden toes
Your raggy coat
Trailing far behind you.
To Ecquador
To Ecquador
And never said goodbye.
When they heard your tulips
Disobeyed you
They looked me in the eye
And stem and leaf
Fell curving to their own
Desire. Would you mind?
I think they bowed in grief
Perhaps rebellion,
Stem and leaf.
But you will never know
For you have gone
To Ecquador
To Ecquador
And I am left behind.

Berta Freistadt

You are so tender

You are so tender
And big,
Like the forty by fifteen
Rhododendron bush at Kew.
There, ten million blossoms
Verging on white,
Yet pink, lilac, rose,
I cannot tell,
Tremble in the wind
Or was it a kiss,
They shrank and blushed
With some delight,
As I leaned to smell
The sweet elusiveness.

So high the bush,
So high you reach
Against my sky
And tremble, quiver,
Sigh, as I
Reach into your strong arms
And up to kiss.

And I
Know your secret beauty too
Have seen you fall back
In wide eyed delight,
Seen you floating in my bed
On a warm tide,
On a cold night.

So in winter will
Twig remember flower,
Remember blossom
That framed your smiling face?
Tho you perhaps

are evergreen to my heart,
Forever flowering
Great and huge,
Forever looming loftily
In my vision,
In my space.

Berta Freistadt

Get your body off my mind

Get your body
Off my mind
I am trying to concentrate
On my life.
On conversation
And politics and
All sorts of things.
Get your body
Off my mind,
It is humming and
Sharp and it
Sings.

Berta Freistadt

Don't call me
pedant

Don't call me pedant
When I cautiously fence
With words.
When I try on
The hats and coats
Of yours
To see how they fit.
While I let them
Play awhile
In my head,
Trying to harmonise.
Soon my own
Will come bursting out
And I will flower
Like a tree,
Words opening off me
Knocking birds
Off branches,
Sending them singing
To the skies.
Then you will
Drown in petals,
Beg me to stop.
And we will spend
All day and night
Picking a sweet crop.

Berta Freistadt

21

You take off your jumper

You take off your jumper
In the hot restaurant
Where cake will not
Assuage my hunger.
You take off your jumper
Over your head
And for a moment
It is armour
You are abandoning.
Your scarred face is pink
From my stored and ungiven kisses.
We are calm.
I disguise quivering
Of hand and voice
With deep breathing
And I see again
That soft place in your neck
And remember other times
Before you scuttled
Crab-like into a hermit shell.
Other times when you
Abandoned your clothes.

Berta Freistadt

Strong thighs astride my chest

Strong thighs astride my chest
your body presses wet against me
draws up passion as we meet and
yes   your hands press down my palms

I watch you seek me out
this powerful mother who
licks her child with passionate tongue
whose urgent fingers
                    touch my lips
                    open my mouth
                    hold your breast to me –
this is the freedom of wild mothering
to choose
to reach for a hand we don't let fall.

And we can hold together in a circle
our bodies cradle an energy
which spills in sweat in breath in cries
and choose to see our faces as we flow.

Caroline Griffin

Elizabeth

Elizabeth – this formality
marks the difference between now & then,
Lizzie – I want to say
we convent schoolgirls were heroic lovers,
unsupported explorers.
What we did put us outside the world we knew
and for a time we held together.

I wanted your certainty
kneeling with you in the church by the river
then watching the floods.
A precise vision I had
the boat slicing through water
wanting to see how it curled   how it
washed the bank
and spread over the pathways.

Remember the world we stepped out of –
the porcelain madonnas   the virtues of silence
men in suits   flickering electric signs –
the boy I kissed on the river-bank
his hand cupping my breast
his leg taut & nervous against mine.
Boys did this & I gave you a warning
trying to say what the world had taught me.

You climb into bed with me
it is impossible to believe   we touch each other
turning away from the world inside me
not that
we were tender   engrossed   but straitened
so straitened   by silence
the narrow bed   your sleeping sister.
We suffered a passion of reaching out
so cramped we bruised each other.
And in the morning the shock

seeing the marks of how we felt
the bruises on our breasts –
we needed wider times.

Remember what they did to us?
Those who were masked –
the teacher walking by who watched us kissing.
The nun whose mask slipped
gripping the table   rising with anger
she asked you what we did –
and searched my poems to find out.

The others used no words.
They did not speak, just sideways sarcasm
and fear. Your phone-call jerked my father's
mocking
'Don't forget to say you love her.'

Did they know more than we did?

Going on for a year
no one took care of us
there were no celebrations.
We were lovers, climbers
held by nothing but our feelings.
We searched for clarity & comfort
and they shook us, shook us badly.

A rope trails still between us
reach out   grasp it   angry –
see what we had & what was taken from us?
Refuse to let it go.

Caroline Griffin

If my life could be simple

If my life could be simple
a brush stroke on a page
you would be there.
And in this shape I make with my hands
you would see a life moving.

river   I want you to touch me
mountain   we hold this space between us
fiercely   mountain   we push against
our hands, our bodies   hold the choice, the space –
ocean   you move on top of me   ocean
your mouth   your tongue presses
choosing again and again   river
I want you to touch me.

Each touch says
     this is how our lives have been
     and this is how we could be.
Each touch makes a life
     more vivid and more possible.
'We are more than we know.'
'There is no such thing as coincidence.'

I bend to kiss your neck   tender says the kiss
tenderness   your powerful shoulders move
reaching towards my breast   you place
my nipple in your mouth   around you
there is all that I can be of mother
here at the edge of you
holding   respectful
You can call this love or work.

Our bodies move   our hands touch
We are more than we know
and meaning rises to meet this touching
creates a new land to walk on
solid surprise at the bend of a river.

I speak of land   but this is creation
how we become more. Our passion breathes
the child in us, not just the past accepted
but the life in us   as vital as
        the kicking baby
        in the amniotic sac –
how can we touch without
        a raging to create
        more space, more life
or knowing that
        tomorrow I can go back
        and trace my footprints?

I want to use all this
gather it up with energy
like a traveller beginning –
knowing the many shrines I've made
to silence fear with beauty.

The passion in my stride contains this fear.
This ground-swell breathing
is what I have despised   it is myself.

I want now to straddle the lashed boards
straining on the waves.
This is not the best I can do
the best is a line of effort
the edge of the waves where the rubble collects –
This is how I move
with you   with myself   to
remember learn and invent.

                              Caroline Griffin

27

Connection

There is a connection between us
which makes me bite.
A threshold of your skin
which puts my hands to grab
and pull
your breasts texture in my palms
edgy with feeling, full, held
grasped.
There is a drag at me that is
your buttocks indentation,
crest each line neat, divided,
my fingers twist into this, itching
charged with flesh; thumb, wrist.
Such a crisp lip to teeth rounded,
no seams – nothing but a lip, juice smooth.
Deer neck, soft nostrils,
bitten into the muscle up from your
back, bitten into again along your
jaw, teeth are the edge of everything
your jaw is the beginning,
crouch neck pushed upwards,
waiting for my swerving teeth,
suction of my mouth, this is a
hook joining us, wrenching us from
separateness,
departing our world, cutting our heels
into living.
Pubic bone crusts against yours small fat
flesh creeps close to tangents that deny,
give way, cool burning lines dagger across
me, slide into your small soft throated
arsehole, touching lines of silver flesh.
This is belly, aching with open limbs,
body that tells you, finger linked and gentle
there is no place yet, my body found
except connection.

Caroline Halliday

28

I moved in my house

I moved in my house, doing nothing special,
just work and pleasure, the usual pattern;
my son was busy, the garden lay stretched
as it should; my friends ran their lives.
It was just a day, like any other;
you know how it is.

I saw her walk by, on the way to her life.
She looked up by chance; I looked back with interest.
We talked for a bit. She went on her way.
the earth went on turning; you know how it is:
just once in a life one can feel the dance.
I went back to my house.

I knew when she knocked, when I opened the door;
I knew when she spoke; I knew when I answered.
I knew how my son would stroke me with questions;
I knew how my friends would see me transfigured;
I knew how the garden had stretched into forest
and jungle and plain.

I knew how we'd listen and wait; I knew
how we'd go on walking towards one another;
I knew how the rain would feel on her hair;
You know how it is; I knew how we'd prosper;
I knew the conditions, the rites and the stages,
the seamless conjunction.

Gillian Hanscombe
Suniti Namjoshi

All the words

All the words have leaped into air like the cards
in Alice, like birds flying, forming, re-
forming, swerving and rising, and each word
says it is love. The cat says it is love.
It says, 'I am and I love.' And the fawn
in the forest who lost his name, he eats
from your hand. He tells you, 'My name is love.'
And all the White Knight's baggage rattles, and cries
it is love. And even the tiger-lily, even the rose
say only that they are themselves. And they say
they are love. All the little words say
they are love, the space in between, the link
and logic of love. And I can make no headway
in this heady grammar, and suddenly
and here, you are, I am, and we love.

Gillian Hanscombe
Suniti Namjoshi

Christ how my circumspect heart

Christ how my
circumspect
heart goes
spinning between beats
throat goes
dry as old bark
blood in my
ears goes banging

so
having undone me
                    will you
gather me kindly
lay
hands on my eyelids
flowers in the
cleft of my breasts

you oh you
have
discovered me
unsealed my longing
appointed me mighty

named me

Gillian Hanscombe
Suniti Namjoshi

Well, then let slip the masks

Well, then let slip the masks
        and all the notes we have taken,
let them fall to the ground and turn into petals
to make more luxurious our bed, or let them
turn into leaves and blow in the air, let them
make patterns, let them amuse themselves.
The curve of your breast is like the curve
of a wave: look, held, caught, each instant
caught, the wave tipping over and we in our bower,
the two of us sheltered, my hands on your thighs,
your body, your back, my mouth on your mouth
and in the hollows of your jaws and your head
nuzzling my breasts. And the wave above us is
folding over now, folding and laughing. Will you
take to the sea, my darling? Will you let me caress you?
The tips of your feet, your legs, your sex?
Will you let my tongue caress you? Will you
lie in my arms? Will you rest? And if the sun
is too strong, should burn too much, will you
walk with me to where the light is more calm
and be in me where the seas heave and are
serene and heave again and are themselves?

Gillian Hanscombe
Suniti Namjoshi

Measure

measure?
may be (and if oh the
will can win or
world can wait or
we can make this oh this
wanting soon abate) may be
if this
luxury will state her
purpose and be gone (may
be and will be when
eyes may see what
makes ears hesitate)

and pleasure?
ah
I (and we) may (can)
always understate
what magnitudes we mean
(with what
weight of waiting now can
(may) the wanting
quiet and the reach relieve)
? yet no not
measure and not
pleasure whom we seek

merely the
ancient matrimonial in
which we
two make what is made

Gillian Hanscombe
Suniti Namjoshi

You're so far away

Let's agree to meet in our dreams
to touch, my love, in time
send kisses with each letter sealed
to bind your wish and mine.
Let's savour the tokens we exchange
linger in the embrace of words
bask in the joys of poetry
lie quiet nights reflecting
on the meeting of dreams.

Iyamide Hazeley

Vanilla Sugar
or
Verse for a
'Hallmark' Greeting Card

Vanilla sugar
sweetie pie
no one more in love
than I

cinnamon cookie
honey bun
you and I have so
much fun

we've no wish for
stronger spices
tricks and traps and
strange devices

we can never
get enough
of the other
kind of stuff

so peppermint candy
sweet cachou
you eat me and I'll
eat you

Joy Howard

You can't go to the Moon
there's no Trains

To wish
for the moon
is so unrealistic
why when there is
a whole round shining earth
to wander
should I dream
for a gleaming chimera
I should be content
to catch her bright reflection
in a pool
and leave her be
delighting in
her mystery
not long
for mastery
politically as well as
poetically
undesirable

Joy Howard

Casablanca Time Again

Shall I have to spend the
                    rest of my life
    saying tearful goodbyes
                        at airports
my first flight I cried
        at take off and on landing
    I couldn't understand it – now
                    I see it as an omen
another plane   another year   another love
        another tear   another goddam
                            airport
                                goodbye

Joy Howard

Another Reading

You write of goats, I curl
in my chair sniffing at mountains.
Your book falls open at the right page
where rock meets water.

I remember how it was to be goat
to clutch at the landslip, drive horned
and headlong at the untouched shape
of legs running, running, see how we run.

Only once to run the gauntlet
scale battlements, send arrows in
scratch at the sullen earth
land's face through a visor named shut.

The letters hold their walls.
Behind their gauze the city celebrates
its myth; your limbs run with light
out of water, out of goat's eyes.

There is only one plunder.
See how the stars hold in their course
in spite of me. I read futures
of crystal where the ink grows thick.

Nicki Jackowska

The Two Nights

And after you have gone
gathering your limbs back
from their sprawl
the knots and riddles of
their expeditions
crossed the small water
sent your grief pitching
down the widening channel
between our separate flesh
(your hand opened)

And after I have peeled
your colours off my linen
shaken the pillow-mould
to neutral
let the wide air take you
only then I tear the first words
from their page
the ones that cut and chipped
against your cheek
language like flint, the
goat-butt that knows no
other definition

Beloved hollows
how we went in armourless
scooped out each seed
caught each blown scent

How the first night you
roared and flooded me
and tossed and pitched my
taut and holding flesh
to curve and contour you

And then again translating
our small wars, its contracts

parries, its crossed swords
we come the second night
to land upon some mountain's
leaping crest

Through that dark, lightning
shifts between my thighs
chasm of light each time
your bulk shifts against me

To moan at anchor
this ship is buffeted and borne
aloft, skidding the waves
I'm buried in your hold
carved and provided
I have all the necessary
balms and incantations
only the storm prevents
our disembarking

The first time I wrote it
my song was barbed and blistering
stripping our careful skins
The first time I tracked it
I turned this way and that
bitching the page

Now the story dips into
its brother underneath
ends on the ocean
with my boat manned
equipped for weather;
beneath, tracking it, the fish
the ocean's eye, marking it
a spume of silver
in our wake

This love goes on daring
its lands; charts our decisions.

Beyond such pages
and today's innocence
our mating multiplies its
muscle; we hold fast
and grow together over water

Nicki Jackowska

Making a Season

I wasn't thinking of snow-hunger
more of a fragile flower-head nodding
stealthy out of its envelope.

My love's a book-length hawkish river
twisting its course. We read trees there
hear where the season drives the raven's croak.

Summer's easy;   it's the stab of the north star
sharp as needles, launching a constellation.

Keep your careful seeds, I'm sparse
as crab-apples in a lean month, holding
the source of rivers underground.

And going home I pluck the sweet
barbs out, skin catching its map.

Not snow-blind, mad on the rampant river
but hoarding where the land grunts
under keel and water, shoving roots on.

Nicki Jackowska

Diary of Days for Adjoa

I am carrying your grin
with me and all your many faces:
imagined face of your teens
loss across your cheek
bones after your abortion
hurt hanging from different angles
over the years I haven't known you;
and your face this morning

You make me travel
past my past
hands raking earth
trusting you enough to
dig for worms or treasures
old dry roots coming unstuck

this land I've found in you
is frightening too
how far might we go
how far could we go

longing does not listen to reason
but trust – need meeting past
and making friends – carries
me buoyant to our next time

I could write you a diary
of days since I last saw you:
how I sang to Ella Fitzgerald
in the car going north east from Brixton
how although love is old
Ella doesn't sing of two black women
watching *Falling in Love* eating
nan and mutter paneer drinking
gin and talk talk talking
till our eyes held onto our fire
till our bodies took over the telling of stories

43

I listened to all Ella's devils
watching for signs and glancing at the map
I never knew I had and
I'd left something behind in Brixton
I carried your grin and your smell
that whole journey wearing your soft yellow
these past days I've caught that smile
at odd hours – you surprising me
you around me, me sometimes wishing
I could let go for a while
stop your dancing in my head

And   I know no definites except
how much I love the caring you bring
the way your eyes travel places and
then suddenly stop and stare
amazed – a comment on our happening

I am missing you it seems so long since
your arms held my need
And still, I don't know
what it is you want
or what it is I want
but I know we will give
each other something
something
like a raging wind
a scorching sun
an echo from the wilderness.

Jackie Kay

Peony

Let me be that huge red peony
for you to sit inside
my lush red–grape coloured petals
sexy full ripe as thick sensuous lips.
I want to give you secret parts of me
travel with you deep into our caves
dark and wet cool and hot
and find the centre
the core that is left when the petals fall off
And I will meet the pain in you
the anger rising in you
challenge pushing forth upwards to meet me.

Desire flows swells on to the banks
in me wanting to sink into you
our essence welcoming each other
spicy as hot pepper sauce
our lips the colour of fresh
strawberries bitten into

All day I was full of longing
in Covent Garden in Clissold Park
whilst we watched the ducks and the morning
sun make shadows shaft and hesitate
on the grass delicate as the light in your eyes

I could feel this longing grow
like a sunflower between my thighs
the want welling up and taking over
my body needing to answer yours

Later I will enfold you
with a promise gentle as an early morning
strong as my longing is

Something sure as our body movements
can savour each herb ooze out

tarragon marjoram mint
each flavour cinnamon and coriander
we can grind wild garlic in our mortar
and nothing has to last forever
not even the cry of pain

and I will land safely in your arms
I don't need an always
but the Now rises and swells
in my throat the Now makes my heart
beat run fingers through my hair
the Now swollen as soaked figs

Remember. Although I am young
my need is fully grown
and no one said you don't long hard when you're young
and no one said you don't hurt past forty.

Jackie Kay

We can try again another day

And still you lie,
a young novice,
with a dark jaw,
dedicated to self-mortification.
Peaceably you say
(gazing through the window
from our bed
at the effortless garden)
we can try again another day.

The adder strikes, strikes again
– you have your sturdy hoe and a simple vow;
where but in the walled monastery
kitchen garden
Brother Alphonso
disinterring with murmuring
of mantras, cabbages
with care
for vital floating winter soup,
and turnips
for the abbey mules.

The devil keeps low
and reveres the habit.
How fearful is Satan
who strikes at the nearest and lowest flashing
object; and dares not
coil high to the saint's wound.
So in retreat is heaven.
So fearful is God.
So still you lie.

Judith Kazantzis

Static

A fortress of static
surrounds me out of the phone.
The charge of the light brigade
remains constant, neither advances
                              nor retreats.

This is a dull relief, like
the settling of my stomach after
that large strawberry I ate last
night; I vegetate; you can't
                    reach me.

And I can't ring you, money
money on another call
to act a touching: my
breasts, your arched tongue that
                    arched me

that bared me like a tide
tongue wriggling sand from stone,
weed waved back from the
running – We can't blow kisses to
                    act that

now this fervent static serves its
impersonal freaks and mistakes.
As we served each other well
and now shamble
                    to halt.

                              Judith Kazantzis

To the Woman in the Office

You'd laugh
If only you knew
The number of times today
I've wanted
To kiss you
The number of times
I've wanted
To hold you
In my arms
The number of times
Your smile
Has left me frozen
And your wit
Hit a nerve
Making me feel
Uneasy
You'd laugh
Because
That would be
The only way
For you
To cope.

Kim

Let's not think about that

Your overtures overjoy me
The hand you're holding is pat
I know you're going to destroy me
But let's not think about that

Let's open up to each other
And see if sex can be fun
Try not to think of your mother
And I won't think of my son

We've got a little spare time
We like each other's looks
And we can have a rare time
Forget about the hooks

Just go ahead and enjoy me
I'll play the mouse to your cat
I know you're going to destroy me
But let's not think about that

Fran Landesman

I Quite Like Men

I quite like men. They're rather sweet
I like to give them things to eat
They have nice hands and charming necks
And some of them are good at sex

My sympathies are feminist
But I am glad that men exist
Although they can be perfect swine
They're nice with candlelight and wine

They warm me up when I feel cold
And some of them have hearts of gold
They irritate me now and then
But on the whole
I quite like men

Fran Landesman

On the State of Englishness
(A Fairy Tale)

An English man fell in love
Oh wildly in love
With a woman whose long Hungarian hair
Spread like the desert
Across her apricot back.
And she returned his love
Her vowels dark and deep and moony
Kissing his suburban nipples
Shamelessly.
He bit his lip and bit his lip
And silenced his heart
And tried not to express . . .
Anything at all.
The effort made him go pink.
And pinker.
Until he turned into an English Rose
And she woke up one morning
To find a pink satin bud
Resting on her belly
As if it had found its true nesting place
At last.

Deborah Levy

Nine Reasons Why

I like your spirit full of loving
I like your words full of sunflowers
I like your fullstops there aint no compromise
I like your commas there's room for persuasion
I like your shirt full of cotton
I like your umbrellas full of jazz
I like your feet tapping truth
I like your politics full of red kisses
I like you lots I really do
In fact I can't help feeling
Squeaky Good When I'm With You!

Deborah Levy

Frolic

Petal
Yasmin
Vlodostk
you are my thin veined madonna

squeezing dialectics from lemons

you are my love
for a century

we celebrate each other with plums
You plant the stone in my heart

Petal
Goyim
Tusika
you are my wide lipped laugh

rowing me out to sea

we find arguments under beds
we bite into almonds

halfmoon maps
to trace later

Petal
Ykipa
Wrazivca
you are my love

We put ice cubes in chypre
Your tears are hot

The century oils its limbs.

Deborah Levy

In Perfect Time

This is the point when we are innocent,
we strip and join at once each time we meet
and bring together every element:
unfallen angels don't have such delight.
The love that moves the sun and other stars,
mute weight of every creature's urgent day,
here reaches speech and at our coming cheers:
poles hold and fold the world, its core this joy.
All well. But we are animals of earth,
whose pulse dictates that static union
is bliss but brief or death. Life must be growth;
kindness can't prevent that separation.
Those who have sometimes tasted paradise
escape, through hope, the pit of bitterness.

Dinah Livingstone

Night Prayers

Her old age
is waiting for her
at the bottom of her mirror.
So she says,
I am not my face,
I will find a lover
to love my soul.

Maybe she cannot control
other people
but really
God is more real
and he will
always
work to rule.

Mirror mirror on the wall
answers her:
In evening pain,
remember Queen,
beware of human breath;
it can kill
a good death.

Dinah Livingstone

Love Poem

You wrote a poem
underneath my skin.
I have lost words before
but I am marked by some.

The street is fat with sun,
we have escaped, you carry me
my mouth blown out by sun.
I have lost words before
but I am marked by some.

You have left, gone into the tinny night.
The dark tastes sour, rich sentences
are falling off my tongue
like lazy little stars.
I have lost words before
but I am marked by some.

Lindsay MacRae

Love Gone Cold

What have we swallowed,
mice or razor blades?
What makes my breath so thick,
must be the cigarettes,
must be the heavy sky
so tight no sun can squeak through.

We should have met
in another time and place
you and I.
We should have met
and merely stuck.

You turn out milky smiles
for the bossy little princess
in your bed, you know this is difficult to write
Sometimes, words are just pretty.

I need some kind of pick-me-up,
another drink, to take the taste,
so I'll be sugar-mouthed or full,
a good square meal would do.

Any drug's efficient in its way.

We stay in bed for hours
waiting for things to break.
Your fingers touch my face.
We have not been so gentle
for so long.

I write, you read,
no book is long enough.
The pre-recorded tape wails on
about love, about love.

You know each tune
is a mean little knife.

Lindsay MacRae

58

Dear John . . .

Loving you was difficult
so I never did.
Ours was a romance
whose flame never flickered
and whose honeyed words never dripped.

You have spilt a pint of Guinness down my front
and asked me to buy you another.
On most of our dates
I have managed to think of a reasonable excuse
not to be present.

Once we sat in your bedroom
you chanted your boy scout motto;
showed me a picture of Roger, the family dog;
and gave me some tips on successful hari-kiri –
all before suggesting we might try sex.

I cannot describe our life between the sheets
because you had a Spiderman duvet.

Your idea of the preliminaries
was to fumble in the dark for your glasses
and ask me if I'd like to try them on.
And you never waited until afterwards
to go to sleep.

I wonder, does the older generation realise
that *you* are the kind of fun it is missing out on.

Lindsay MacRae

59

True Life Romance

I used to fall in love with pop stars
I pinned their lovely faces to my wall,
then I found out when you've slept with one pop star
you've slept with them all.

Imagine the après-gig glow,
I bought him a drink and I really enjoyed the show.
The way he thundered masterfully
through every ripped-off riff he knew
told me he'd been practising for years.

He disappeared to the toilets several times
and came back with the early symptoms of a cold –
but did he ever offer me any? No.
I was thrilled by the thought of being on the arm
of someone slightly famous and very drunk.

He whisked me off to a quiet little restaurant he knew
in Tottenham Court Road
(where he was sure he'd be recognised)
I ordered the best doner kebab, with trimmings,
he wasn't hungry so he had
three litres of Kolossi Castle wine to take away.

And as he lurched towards the door
with a far-away look on his face he said:
'You comin' then Carol?'
I reminded him that Carol was not my name
he said that Carol was the name of his first love
before the fame came
and that I looked a bit like her.

All night at the movies,
it was *Ghostbusters* all night.
His lips brushed my ear,
I felt the moist delight of an old belch
and those three little words –
'Pass the wine.'

We watched the dawn rise over King's Cross
and went to his room without view.
He invited me in for a breakfast drink
and (if he was up to it)
a screw.

My head reeled, my heart beat quick and fast
was he to be my first pop star or my last.

Would my name be the refrain in a love song of passion and
   pain.
Would this night be the start of a permanent place in his heart.
Would I be able to go on the road with him,
split up after five stormy years and sell my memoirs to a
   Sunday rag.
Would he launch a charity appeal,
be knighted, marry me in a fit of respectability
and settle down in a country mansion
while I presented a weekly pop programme, wearing a
   designer frock.

Probably not. So I went home.

Lindsay MacRae

The Immaculate Conception

The good thing about an immaculate conception
is that it doesn't come to your bed pissed
and it doesn't stain the sheets.

In fact the only thing wrong
with an immaculate conception
is that it's always preceded
by a huge great angel
who leaves the light on.

Lindsay MacRae

Ms World

Can you imagine
the howls of ridicule
jeers, hoots of contempt
as we stand there
she and I
on the glittering stage
her wearing the sash for Germany
and me for England.

We haven't got
the right shaped bottoms
neat and tight thirty-five inches
and Miss Germany's
breasts are too big
and Miss England's too small
to fit the thirty-six B that
every beauty queen must have.

Her waist is not slim
and my stomach
sags a little since I had two babies;
her legs are short and I have no ankles.
But . . . just imagine
that her mouth smiles
inviting you inside
to allow you to know her.

Imagine if you can
her dark blue eyes
thick lashed full brimmed
with tears.

Know our quiet laughter
if you are near us
recognise us as we move
with wholeness
to the music

of our women-only discos
free from male stares
and man-made images
of women's bodies.

Just imagine us singing
heads thrown back
our laughter loud now
in the September sunshine.

And think again
from whence
comes women's beauty.

Caeia March

Passion

What does passion know?
Passion knows nothing
It is red and blind
And plays the congas
With the accuracy of a brain
surgeon.

Passion lives in the heat
It is Irish and confused
It wears a sodden shirt
And plays the double bass
With the fingers of an angel.

Passion speaks in gibberish
It is lost and lonely
It wears broken shoes
And plays the saxophone
With water streaming down its face.

Passion is clever
It is full up and hearty
It wears a leather belt
And sings like a face full of sun
Passion knows everything.

Sue May

Haircut

I've been restless today
Either there's going to be a storm
Or I'm going to write a poem
Can't get you out of my mind
Haven't washed my hair since you touched it
That's true, you touch me sometimes unexpectedly
I'd just had it cut, so you smelt it
Like a friendly dog, a labrador
I don't think of you as a dog.
I think of you as a magician.

Sue May

Photograph

I always take one you don't expect
I called you to face me
and in a flash this happened:
you looked at me
one eyebrow raised, not smiling
honestly quite tired,
arms folded, tolerating me
There's a six-foot skinhead behind you
being cheeky, drinking coffee
He's your responsibility –
him and his evo-stik.
The high street is full of worried people
and everyone blames you.
I will press like a flower
this torn out image.

When the prints come back
you want this one
because it's true.

Sue May

There'll Be No Better

How coldly the moon stands above the garden.
And yet I like this square – the tall trees moving,
The homeliness of lawn and its enclosures.
You are asleep . . . The bedroom and the garden
Are almost one, as the glass door swings open.

This is our happy time; there'll be no better.
World will sunder or split – or we merely grow older.
The moon shines brightly: I half fear the future.

Gerda Mayer

Chopin's Minute Waltz

First love
who played it
with learner fingers
                              slow ten
                    der notes drif
                                    ting in
                    to the garden . . .

Gerda Mayer

The Old Wife Speaks

Only in sleep
are you still most tender;
        perhaps
dreaming me young again . . .

Gerda Mayer

The Stone-hitter

Two thimblefuls of wine, and slightly later
The ribbon-like passage of a sea-going cloud
Forces his brow on mine.

His mouth is a contested
Road juncture,
His lips are hasty slashes,
My dropped waist slips
To a rougher world of six-foot clouds.

Medbh McGuckian

Girls in the Plural

The shadow of a summer tightly folded
Fitted without violence over the shoulders
And breasts of separating roses, though no one
Was passing the window.

I let it lie there a twelvemonth,
A wistful, clinging letter,
Reflected in my mirror, listening to my clock,
As one who had never given herself to him,
But found herself with child, and frittered
Away the thoughtless wind that grew in her
Like some deflowered ghost.

Lost days, while far away
Cells were ordered otherwise.

My closed eyes had just made up
That simile about his eyes awakening,
The colour of their fear, a promise halved.
I had ransacked the world for stained
Wings of the same possessive fabric,
But none of my removals
Was in any sense a flight.

More the invention of a new caress
Wearing off like pain unmixed
With the round poems, the edged tools,
Pressing like a damaged cloud against the doors.

Elsewhere, he
Breathed in the air that belonged to me.

Medbh McGuckian

Death of a Ceiling

The sounds that shapes make in the air,
The shapes that sounds make, matter
Whenever a stone or pocket-knife
Is rocketed through water.

So lightning arranges the logarithms
Of ferns, equates the radius
Of the moon to the number of breaths
We draw in an hour.

The flowers of the past
Closed with an endless flickering.
Even after the outer petals
Lit up like a line of lamps,
The kiss of the other day
Was the one they were most against.

And yet it could only have lain
In wait, like the decorous seeds
Of the sunflower – each spiral brighter
By four more than that within.

I thought so darkly down
My left arm of a voice-coloured
Garden he has blundered upon,
Once or twice, I got the dead
Lavender away. How long

Will that garden be a garden?
As long as the picture spoken
By the window makes no claim
To be any closer a branch-pattern
Than glass should be.

And the rooms that were all paragraphed
By either a step up or down,
I should have entirely papered
With used postage stamps:

Their leaf-mould letting out the house
Into a red linen, quaker brown,
Brew of so many fruits between
The element that suits him, and mine.

Medbh McGuckian

Differences

he speaks to me of other things,
like cracks in the wall,
and spills on the floor,
and I've lost a plastic spoon this week
And *somebody* left the fridge door open
and the ice all melted

(the potatoes were raw tonight
like the fish
i'd set the oven
forgot to light it)

my face creases, I cry at the sink
I do not believe this mountain I live with
i want to talk of other things
like death and life
and the failure of post–war planning
and how can we go on together
like this

and he says let's make the shelves
let's pretend
let's play at house
mummies and daddies
happy
together

Kath McKay

Kite-flying

years I've waited for this
and I never understood their fascination
whole shops devoted to their art,
magazines, conventions,
thousands of chinese kites in blue chinese skies.

I unroll the string and walk,
then a quickening in my stomach; –
one tug, a bounce on air,
and I am hooked for ever.

I had forgotten such uncertainty
my groin aches a memory
of that high mewing call
searching for the hilly wooded country
as it picks my spirit clean

and I can walk on water now
dance the tightrope and soar upwards,
screeching ever louder
'I want higher'.

Kath McKay

The Unmarked Ceiling

It sounds as if it's raining
                finally
the rain that the skylight's
waited for all day

takes me back to the night
I got home to find him crying
and the water pouring in

It was only the first of a run
of sudden storms
while we tried to get a builder
and a price
for the reslating

keeping paint cans and pans
on the floor
in different places

I still think there is one
inexplicable
point
where the water comes down
from an indoors landing

a hole which isn't healed
because it isn't
in the roof

This is the spot I'm drawn to
in my dreams
when it falls from a ceiling
totally unmarked
in a house which may be
yellow
more extensive
but is this one

and leaks even though
outside
it isn't raining

Mary Michaels

At times

At times
I empty myself
a wilful cry for the temporary
and there creeps in a cold fear
of threshold emptiness
something
that needs filling
till I am watching
your warm head
a glow behind the chords

Your fingers trace
the string-held keys
of moments
when
a wave
like cushioned cosiness
passes temporarily
to reassure
and I am pacified
by the brief thought
that maybe there is no need to hurry
to worry

a flicker, like a chance
if we choose
a lifetime could be ours
and the icy hand
of wilfulness
is mine
and longs to warm
between the sheets.

Cheryl Moskowitz

Another Woman

Your voice on the telephone
is thin as wire.
I say hello – what else? – and
can I speak to . . . ?
I give you my name – what else?

I could tell you how
you have fattened, these last weeks
inside my skin;
fragments of you filled out with guesswork
to life size, the size of my own life.

I could tell you: you too
fought for breath before you knew it
and later
you went on throwing open your married windows
to learn to love gusts of cold.

Then in I came
whistling to keep up my courage
and yours, I hoped, and instead made you shiver.
I shiver myself
most days.

But if you answered
no, that was never me, no
it doesn't feel like that to me at all;
you could talk on
while I practised listening.

Thinly, you say
he hasn't got back yet from . . . I'll
tell him you called.
Yes, I have to agree, thank you –
what else?

Rosemary Norman

80

Waterloo Station

We clung together an hour,
walked, talked,
laughed in earnest;
above the river, the sky
lay wide open and blue as ice.

Back under the station roof
words became plain,
practical, and our tongues
(for Waterloo would part us)
soon tired of them and turned to touching.
A hundred stares
faded as we kissed, unless
it was we who were absent.

I am alone here now.
This is again the most public of places
and my mouth
the most private of parts.

Rosemary Norman

Demon-lover

This room is not for staying
nor for stopping
nor for rest

It is for holding one's breath
in the doorway, without striking
a light

without pausing to look

It is a hall of black mirrors
shone by eyelight and scented
with fear

Beneath scattered love letters
I rummage around to find a boot

That slipped off your cloven hoof
and was left behind
in this room

Sylvia Paskin

Bi-lingual

Between him and me, I feel
like a bi-lingual dictionary
I'm sliced each time in half
by an alphabet which begins
with L. L for L O V E that is.
Believe me, I've really tried
to talk to him, to communicate.
I've tried to talk to him in
silhouettes, in shadow play,
fluid and staccato, my hands
dipping and weaving and curving
like outraged maddened birds.
There are no equivalents.
There are no translations.
I've seen the frontier that is
difference divide us this way
and that. Divide my continent
like a line of stitches on bare
skin, like a line on a map.
It's possible that there is a
sailboat that would take us
back to the lost islands of
fantasy but I don't know which
side I'm on any more. I lean
back in my chair and make him
look at me. I refuse to travel
further. It's love, but it's
a pity . . .

Sylvia Paskin

Without a beginning nor an end

without a beginning nor an end
wide nets of stars move in and
out of place. Silent in the
moonlight, the lovers are sleeping
under a robe of antelope. Under
the animal skin they are tender
and near each other's hands.
Their bones too shine tenderly
through the skin's transparence.
They are sleepers, they are dreamers
carried from one dream to another,
these lovers, weightless in each
other's arms. The plains too are
dreaming, silent in the moonlight,
dreaming their own dream, like lovers
without a beginning nor an end

Sylvia Paskin

We are Welcome

We unlock the door
The joy of this safe space
Greets us.
We who are used
To sirened streets
Gradually trust
The green bird song.
She who owns this place
A past lover
Who moved gently on
Kisses me when we meet
Lends me the key
Of her rural sanctuary.
Now the woman in my life
Leans into the silence
As she welcomes my body
Her wanting fingers
Ease out my cramps
Tightness rolls away
Eyes full of her landscape
Giving me my body back
Langourous and elastic
Ready to welcome her.

Sue Sanders

Love Poem

My love
the sun
s
  e
   t
    s
in your eyes
and
    s
    e
   s
  i
 r
golden
in your body.

Valerie Sinason

Ghostly Love

In the quiet time
when the dead rest under wet leaves
I call to you under skin and sheets
Come now – it is safe to come.

But who lies wet and curled
in the arms of the dead?
Who will not will not let go
of the drifting blossom?
Who screams down the emptying branches
of storm-fast trees?

Who
trapped in earth and blinded with green
holds fast to the dead
and will not will not
come to me

Valerie Sinason

Jealousy

At the crossroads
a man and woman are kissing

I pass them morning and night
the man stretches out his left hand
her right arm passes through air

It is necessary to remember these things
it is necessary to take account
the glass is advancing

Sometimes I leave my house a cunning way
Sometimes I go out in disguise
with clouds as bandages

At the crossroads
a man and woman are kissing
the air closes like a mouth

It was not my arrangement
it was not in my appointments diary
it is not on the black road sign
above the moving crossroads

The crossroads move
night and day
the man and woman follow me
a trail of red mouths

They cannot reach me now
they cannot see me
this blurred sky is their breath
on the glass that divides us.

Valerie Sinason

Nuclear Unit

She dressed his words in
soldier's uniform
and sent them goosefleshing
along his leg

He disguised her silences
as lemmings
and opened wide
the sea of his mouth

She hijacked his mind
behind a tight clench
of thighs

He lamed white horses,
drowned mermaids,
beheaded queens.

She kicked
superman in the prick
had an arrangement
with Samson's barber

He planted bombs
in her skull
and watched her thoughts
explode

And when the bombed cities of
their eyes wept black over the
ruins of their bodies

Still their love stuck
seared
sucked their brains

A mushroom cloud
rising in their skulls

Valerie Sinason

The Dance

Arms
spiral
in clinical
cold
repetitions.

Spiritless
a
piercing wind
blows cobwebs
out
of
suspended
animation.

And on
the off
beat
a
mellow
voice
chides

push me
push me
push me

over
the edge
but
catch me.

Even ebony
may shatter
if dropped
from a
significant height.

Maud Sulter

Full Circle

Locating the anger
as it wells up
in my body
skull back thighs
feet – I ground
myself.

Letting go
of the hatred
the angry fur–ball
a putrid mass
of unresolved conflict
that ate away cancerously
at myriad points in my body.

Brought into clear
vision the immediate
realisation
that I have no need
for either you
or your culture
they have nothing
of value
to offer
me now.

I affirm my own space
under the baobab tree
in my father's garden
black to black
spirit to spirit
connections.

Maud Sulter

Touching heartsease

my little pretty patch of wilderness
hung in the short term
between desire and passion
turgid with flowers –
broad iris buds,
drift of forget
me nots
mazy with sleep
drawn deep across rain
falling soft
warm silent
in a deepening green

today no edges are visible
colour melts back
this is a veiny petal
place
warm laved under tree
before sun
wet with translucence

we wait here without memory
swimming and drowning
touching heartsease
and approaching
honesty

Janet Sutherland

Leaning over

Leaning over
to press a little row of
judas kisses
down the length of the spine
he smiles
and tries to remember
her name.

Janet Sutherland

Variegation

By late evening she was cleaning the
sink . . .

off-white at the periphery
– the character of Ivy
depends on a smooth edge

using bleach on the tea stains
carefully, to avoid splashing her hands

on newer stems
this portion of the leaf
is cream
gradually fading with age

she poured a generous measure
down the plughole

variegation is effected
by the grouping together
of different pigments
– light green / dark green,
in some cases
red or other exotic colours

wiping the brass fitting round it
till it shone

two shades of green, quite distinct
and separate,
the darker laid over the fairer

remembering Jim and the young girl
fucking on the spare bed

older leaves lose clarity, gain depth:
greygreen, they are trees in a landscape
further away than you thought

94

she sees him in the mirror over
the sink and says without
turning –
can I trust you?

Janet Sutherland

Cat got your tongue?

Cat got your tongue?
they'd say
and mother would help
dishing out words
with comfortable ease
not quite   but near enough

now the mind falters
seeing your lips
smiling   mouthing
the phrase that is less
than not quite

'picture' was the object
so 'it hangs on a wall
and you look at it
it has a frame and it
imagines something that is
not quite'

but more than
this is the shy tongue
talking by parable (?)
we look at each other
piling up names
reaching past
i would kiss you.

Janet Sutherland

To the spider in the crevice
behind the toilet door

i have left you four flies
three are in the freezer next to the joint of beef
the other is wrapped in christmas paper
tied with a pink ribbon
beside the ironing table in the hall
should you need to contact me
in an emergency
the number's in the book
by the telephone.

p.s.   i love you

Janet Sutherland

Lover

I don't just want
your heart
I want your flesh,
your skin
and blood and bones,
your voice, your thoughts
your pulse
and most of all your
fingerprints,

everywhere.

Nothing is more criminal
than love,
it steals hours from
the day,
dreams from my head,
the sun
from the sky,

perhaps it shone today,

I don't recall,
I distilled all your words
and made my own climate.

Isobel Thrilling

Leaving

Your moon face
grinning inanely
is on the wane already

no safety belt
between you
and a shattered horizon.

You pull away
and my clasp
snaps open

these days alone
loom more dangerous
than a motorway.

Jenny Vuglar

siren song

i want you in the warm
tide and the tug of the undertow   i want
you wet and willing   i
want you

(don't be afraid   this is a different
trick and one those sailors never
understood)

i want you all
over me   i want you soft and
spread out laughing   sinking and
sucked into me   breathing
water and loving every
minute of it   i want you drowning
in my arms
            (i want you to want
me this
way too)

i want you in the slip and
slide of the undertow   i want
you to forget the dangerous
rocks and come diving with me into deep
water   i want you
wet and willing   warm and
deep deep
down in me
            i want to
drown myself in
you

Marg Yeo

100

jumping into joy

reaching to light my cigarette your hand
trembles   i know you are
tired and not so well   but still a wave of
wanting swoops up my
belly
        it sticks
hard in the back of my throat
though   so i don't catch your
hand   i don't
run my hand down and over into your soft
palm   i don't shift
chairs to the empty one i've in a moment of
caution barricaded myself with   i don't
run my fingers slow along your
arm or through your hair

in fact i don't
do anything but watch
you   self-conscious in dark
glasses   telling me this and
that about yourself
                and i don't
know what's the
matter with me   i don't
want you to go   and i kiss
you goodbye just that fraction of a second
longer than i ought
to   for discretion
                but i don't
turn and watch you
disappearing and i don't turn and
chase you up the road and catch your
arm and turn you to
face me   and i don't
say what i'm
thinking

101

back at
work   my knees
buckle   i'm just
jelly   but there's a
crisis   i have to
pull myself together   whip
myself into shape and get
on with it

          all afternoon
though and deep into the evening till i
drift into sleep   you keep
sweeping all over me and i can
see i'm in over my
head already and that it's deep
water
          but for
me   and i hope you
agree   it feels like
jumping into joy

Marg Yeo

getting wise

i am not
alone
you are not
alone
we are not
alone
        listen to me
we are not
alone   we have
each other

think of a spider
woman   (don't shudder)   i mean a
woman spinning and
weaving   very old and
wise   weaving a
web   and each strand   each
filament is a woman

each filament is a spider
woman   and *she*
is spinning and weaving and
so on
        think of
that   nights when the
wind leans in   the cold
grinds at your bones and even the
cat's gone without saying
goodbye
                think of that in the heart
sick empty evenings you rattle
through like a bad
penny in a pig   unspent
unpolished   unattended

think of that

and take a hard
look next door down the
road   not far   just
over the way
              i tell you she'll
be there

          down my
road she shovels a
broom down the gutter   leans a long
arm   swoops up a beer can and
comes right up to meet my
eyes
      don't tell me about
snakes   she is a spider
woman   she is
spinning and weaving   she has the
bluest eyes

don't tell me about getting
old   sister   i'm not getting
old   i'm getting
wise

                              Marg Yeo

O.K.

The day the world was O.K.
Bus drivers took people right to their doors
Milkmen left extra pintas free
Electricity bills were signed:
      'Love and Kisses, L.E.B!'
My dog stopped barking at the postman and wagged her tail
And you loved me unconditionally.

Ann Ziety

Biographical Notes

Sara Boyes was born in 1945, and has mainly worked in theatre as an actress. She has regularly contributed to poetry magazines, is in a women's writing group and performs poetry as a member of the 'Vera Twins'. Married with a child, she lives in London.

Janet Dubé was born in 1941 near the Thames, and went to school even nearer. She was sometimes sent to play near the Avon, and caught sticklebacks in the Wye. While living a little too far from the Severn, her dog fell in a canal. She has lived for ten years between the Teifi and the Towy and can hear the Talog when the wind drops. She collects postcards.

Amanda Eason was born in Essex in 1959, but was brought up in New Zealand. In 1983 she graduated from Auckland University with an M.A. in English. While there she was active in theatre and debating. She has worked variously as librarian, gardener, tutor, waitress and park ranger. Since 1985 she has lived in London and taught English.

Berta Freistadt lives in London. She writes and works as a supply teacher to support this. She is also a lesbian.

Caroline Griffin: 'I'm a white feminist lesbian, born in 1950 in the Midlands and with three sisters. I live in a women's house, co-parenting a daughter (I'm a non-biological mother) and teaching in a boys' comprehensive school. I've begun co-writing plays with Maro Green – *More* (1987) and *The Memorial Gardens* to be produced by Gay Sweatshop in the same year.'

Caroline Halliday: 'Lesbian/MOTHER (= an oppression)/ writer/white m.c./ally to children and adults w. disabilities/ exploring artist. 'Creativity = ALL of these + LINKS/OVERLAP/exploration between them = my (political) WORK (when possible!) D.o.b. 4/7/47.'

Gillian Hanscombe was born in Melbourne in 1945. Her books include *Hecate's Charms* (1976) *Rocking the Cradle* (with Jackie Forster, 1981) and *Between Friends* (1983).

Iyamide Hazeley received a Minority Rights Group/Minority Arts Advisory Service award for poetry in 1984. She was a joint winner of the GLC Black Experience Filmscript Competition in 1986. Her poems have appeared in *Watchers and Seekers*, edited by Rhonda Cobham and Merle Collins (1987).

Joy Howard 'spent far too many of her 40 plus years neither living as a lesbian nor writing poetry. Things are getting better all the time which just goes to show. She is also an incurable optimist.'

Nicki Jackowska has published four collections of poetry, the latest being *Gates To The City* (1985). She has published three novels, including *The Road To Orc* (1985) and *The Islanders* (1987). These poems are taken from a fifth poetry collection, *Africas*.

Jackie Kay was born in Edinburgh in 1961, and brought up in Glasgow. Her poems have been published in *A Dangerous Knowing: Four Black Women Poets* (1983) and *Angels of Fire Anthology of Radical Poetry* (1986) and her short stories in *Everyday Matters 2* (1984) and *Stepping Out* (1986). Her first play, *Chiaroscuro*, was performed by the Theatre of Black Women in 1986.

Judith Kazantzis: 'I'm in my mid-forties, have lived in South-East England forever except recently when experimenting with life inside the empire heartland, just – at Key West, Florida. These love (sic) poems you could find more of in *Let's*

108

Pretend, my third poetry book (1984).'

Kim was born of Irish parents in South Ruislip in 1961. She studied Social Sciences and Administration at London University. She aims to be well known as a dyke writer/performer because she thinks that women need access to work with a positive lesbian bias. She lives alone with her lover and two dogs.

Fran Landesman, poet and lyricist, has written for Broadway, the West End, T V and radio. She has performed in cabaret and on the BBC. Born in the U S , she prefers London.

Deborah Levy has written poems, plays and short stories. Her work for the theatre includes *Pax* and *Our Lady* for the Women's Theatre Group, *Clam, Ophelia and the Great Idea*, and most recently *Heresies* for the R S C . Her short stories include 'A Little Treatise on Sex and Politics' for *London Magazine* and 'The Sinful Twins' for *Women's Review*.

Dinah Livingstone gives frequent performances of her poems in London and elsewhere. Her poems have been published in magazines and anthologies (*Arts Council, P E N , Apples and Snakes, Eve before the Holocaust, Arts for Labour, Publishing for People, Angels of Fire*, and in pamphlets (Katabasis). She received Arts Council Writer's Awards in 1969, 1975 and 1978. Her most recent titles are *Love in Time* (1982), *Glad Rags* (1983), *Something Understood* (1985) and *Saving Grace: New and Selected Poems* (1987).

Caeia March was born on the Isle of Man in 1946. She has had several stories published, including in *Girls Next Door* (1985) and *Everyday Matters Vol 1* (1982), and is the the author of *Three Ply Yarn* (1986). She has lived alone as a lesbian since 1980 and works part time as a clerk for the local council as well as teaching creative writing in Brixton.

Sue May was born in London in 1955. Some of her poems have been published in various magazines and anthologies, including *Angels of Fire* (1986) and *B Flat, Bebop, Scat* (1986). She also writes short stories, reviews and articles.

Gerda Mayer was born in 1927 in Karlsbad, Czechoslovakia and came to England in 1939. Her publications include *Monkey on the Analyst's Couch* (1980), which was a Poetry Book Society Recommendation, and *The Candy-Floss Tree* (1984).

Medbh McGuckian was born in 1950 in Belfast. She is the current writer in residence at Queen's University, Belfast. Her books include *The Flower Maker* (1982) and *Venus And The Rain* (1984). She is married with three sons.

Kath McKay was born in Liverpool and now lives in London. She is a freelance journalist and writes prose and poetry.

Mary Michaels' work has appeared in numerous magazines and anthologies, most recently *No Holds Barred* (1985) and *Angels of Fire* (1986). Three collections of her poetry have appeared: *In Bédar* (1979), *Twelve Poems* (1983) and *The Ice Land* (1985). She lives in London.

Cheryl Moskowitz was born in Chicago, Illinois in 1959 and came to Britain in 1970. She studied developmental psychology at Sussex University. As well as writing poetry, she also writes plays and short stories. Her work has appeared in *Purple and Green* (1985) and *Angels of Fire* (1986). She has also been a member of the Angels of Fire poetry collective. She is married with one daughter and works as an actress.

Suniti Namjoshi was born in Bombay in 1941. Her books include *Feminist Fables* (1981) *From the Bedside Book of Nightmares* (1984) and *The Conversations of Cow* (1985).

Rosemary Norman: 'I was born in London in 1946, and don't remember a time when I didn't write poetry. But I've written harder and better since I've been in a women's writing group. Last year we produced a booklet of our poems, *You're Sweet, You're Speedy*. I live in London with my son, and work as a librarian'.

110

Sue Sanders: 'Born in London in 1947 of middle-class W A S P parentage. An only child. Became a dyke at twenty-one and discovered the women's movement five years later. Trained as a drama teacher and worked with a wide range of women both in London and Sydney. Passionately interested in feminist theatre and have worked with and directed various women's theatre companies.'

Valerie Sinason was born in London and currently works as a child psychotherapist. She has had over a hundred poems anthologised in various books and magazines including *Ambit, The Literary Review* and *One Foot On The Mountain* (1979). She is a regular performer of her work and edits the poetry magazine *Gallery* as well as being a member of Greater London Arts Writers in Schools Scheme. Her first full-length collection of poetry was published in 1987.

Maud Sulter 'blackwomanwriter · born · Glasgow Scotland · 1960 · first poetry collection · *As A Blackwoman* · Akira Press · 1984 · presently lives in London · continues to write · research · reclaim.'

Janet Sutherland was born in Salisbury in 1957. Her poems have appeared in various books and magazines including *Angels of Fire* (1986). She reviews poetry for *City Limits* magazine and works part time for London Borough of Hackney Housing Benefits department.

Isobel Thrilling began writing 17 years ago after recovering from a serious eye operation. Seven of her poems were filmed by Yorkshire television and she has contributed to various magazines including the *Royal Astronomical Society Journal*. Her collection *The Ultrasonics of Snow* was published in 1985.

Jenny Vuglar was born in New Zealand in 1954. She has been living in London since 1979; she is a part-time mother/writer/gardener and lives in a housing cooperative in South London. She has been in a women's writing group since 1981 and has been published in *Spare Rib, City Limits, Wild Words, Iron, Writing Women* and other magazines.

111

At 40, *Marg Yeo* was convinced she was never going to fall head over heels in love. At 40 and 6 months she discovered, once again, that she was wrong.

Ann Ziety is a performance poet who appears regularly in cabaret throughout London. She teaches creative writing in Woolwich and is a member of the Apples and Snakes Poetry Cabaret Collective. She is a small, nervous person who lives in a council flat on Thamesmead with a small, nervous dog.